Contents

Assembly Tomorrow
for Key Stage 2

INTRODUCTION

Coming up with new and interesting ideas for assembly can often be an extremely difficult and time-consuming task. Ideally, of course, the subject matter of every assembly should have a clear moral message, should be motivating for pupils and should be of a broadly Christian outlook. These guidelines were followed in the predecessor to this book, *Assembly Today*, and are also adhered to in this book where we include a new range of assembly ideas appropriate for all children regardless of their faith or cultural heritage.

The assemblies are arranged in school term order, although many can be used at other times in the school year as well. Each assembly has a moral or thought-provoking message (outlined under the 'AIM' heading), a visual or physically active element, a prayer and a suggested song or hymn.

For most of the assemblies you will need an overhead projector. In some instances, where the assembly is based on a story, we have provided silhouettes that need to be photocopied on to paper and then cut out (before the assembly) for display on the OHP. This creates a simple shadow puppet show that is certain to gain the children's full attention! For other story-based assemblies, a simple picture is provided that can be photocopied on to acetate and placed on the OHP to act as a visual aid while the story is being read out. If you have plenty of preparation time, you could involve the children in the retelling of the story or they could even role-play the issues being addressed.

For some of the assembly ideas, you might simply want to follow the script (shown in italics) that is provided on the teacher's page, while for others you might decide to read the assembly notes first and then present it in your own words. Whichever style of presentation you choose, assemblies should be an enjoyable and thought-provoking experience for all concerned.

Andrew Brodie: Assembly Tomorrow KS2 © A&C Black Publishers Ltd. 2008

What's in the shapes?

 AIM: To encourage observation and to gain a valuable message for the day.

PREPARATION

■ If you are planning to use an OHP, photocopy 'What's in the shapes?' (page 4) on to an acetate sheet. This is a very visual assembly in which pupils will need to look and listen attentively.

▦ INTRODUCTION

Introduce the assembly by saying something like:

Today you are going to need to look and listen really well. I am going to show you some shapes, which have words written in them, then ask you some questions about them.

▦ ASSEMBLY

Turn on the OHP and give the pupils a short while to look at the screen.

Who can tell me what word is written in the square but not in any of the other shapes?

Accept responses but don't be surprised if you don't get the correct answer straight away!

So, we have found the first word 'I'. We need to remember that 'I' is the first word.

Ask the child who said the word to remember it ready for later, and do the same as each word is identified correctly.

Now, what word is in the triangle and the circle but not in the square?

Hopefully, the children will find the word 'must'. 'Must' is the second word.

What word is in the circle but not in any other shape? Accept responses.
The third word is 'do'.
What word is not in any of the shapes? Accept responses.
So, we know that the fourth word is 'something'.
Which word is in the triangle but not in any other shape? Accept responses.
The fifth word is 'good'.
What word is in all three shapes? Accept responses.
Now that we have found all the words, could the people who had to remember them stand up and say them in order? Could we have said the words in a different order?

Allow the children some time to consider the words. They should be able to see that 'today I must do something good' or even 'I must, today, do something good' could be created. Ask the children to think up examples of good deeds that they could do. Hopefully, there will be a variety of suggestions ranging from simple actions such as holding the door open for somebody to more elaborate gestures such as washing up for Mum! Once the children have heard some examples and have understood that they can be quite simple, they should be able to think of lots more. You may like to set up a display board of 'good things I can do today'.

▦ REFLECTION

We need to think about what we can do today that is good. The rule is it has to be good for somebody else! We could decide to help somebody else at school or at home. Can you think of good things to do? They can be quite ordinary things or quite special things.

Prayer

Dear God,
Please help us to think of others and how we can do good things for them. Help us all to do something good today. Give us ideas of good things we can do, today and every day.
Amen

Song   Hands to work and feet to run (Someone's Singing Lord, 21: *A&C Black*)

What's in the shapes?

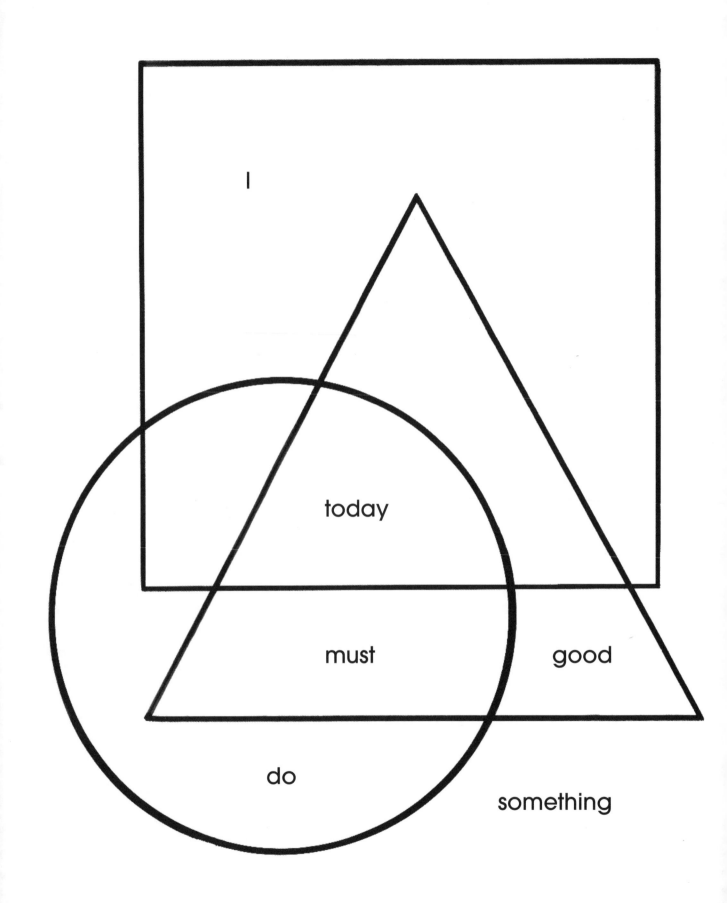

Finding treasure

 AIM: To realise that working hard gets the best results.

PREPARATION

- Photocopy 'Finding treasure' (page 6) on to stiff paper or card then cut out the characters ready to make a simple puppet show on the OHP.
- Read through the assembly so that you can spot where to use each of the silhouettes.

INTRODUCTION

Ask children to indicate by a show of hands whether they know what treasure is. Accept and discuss responses, including the idea that we tend to think of treasure being lots of valuable items such as gold, silver, diamonds and other jewels or perhaps we think of it as lots and lots of money.

Today we are going to listen to one of Aesop's fables. It's all about finding treasure.

STORY

A long time ago an old, old farmer lay dying. He had had a good life and, although he wasn't rich, he had always been comfortable and able to give his two sons everything they needed. However, in recent months, the farm hadn't been doing so well – the crops grew but not as well as they had done when he was younger. He called his two sons to his bedside. "There is treasure buried on this farm," he said. "You must find it."
Not long after this the farmer died.

The two sons were very sad that their father had died but they were also excited about the thought of treasure. They decided to start looking for it straight away and so they went out into the fields very early in the morning and they ploughed and dug all day. They did this every day for weeks and weeks but they didn't find the treasure.

"We're never going to find it," said the older son. "We'd better just plant the seeds as usual then we can start searching again after we have harvested the grain in the autumn."

So they planted the seeds and every day they went out and hoed the weeds and watered the young plants. They had never worked so hard but they enjoyed it because they could see the crops growing well.

When the autumn came they harvested all the crops and discovered they had a better yield than they had had for years. When they took the produce to market they sold it easily and made plenty of money.

"This is amazing," said the older brother. "Father was right. There was treasure buried on this farm and we did have to find it."

REFLECTION

Why did the father say there was treasure on the farm? Why did he say it was buried? What was the treasure? What do you think the moral of the story is?

Encourage the pupils to recognise that the treasure was both the money that the sons made and also the pleasure of seeing their plants growing so successfully.

Do you think there is pleasure in treasure? Sometimes lots of money may be treasure but it may not bring pleasure. Hard work and seeing the results of that hard work can bring a lot of pleasure, so perhaps that is the best treasure to have.

Prayer

Dear God,
Please help us to work hard and to find the treasure in the enjoyment and satisfaction and success that our hard work brings us.

Amen

Song

The building song (Alleluya, 59: *A&C Black*)

Finding treasure

Positive characteristics

 AIM: To think about positive and negative characteristics.

> **PREPARATION**
> ■ Photocopy 'Positive characteristics' (page 8) ready to present on an OHP.
> ■ Cover the lists with a piece of paper so that you can reveal some of the words before others.

■ INTRODUCTION

I am going to ask you to look at some words today. We're going to look at four words on the left-hand side of the screen. For each of those words there are four words written alongside it. Your job is to find the word that goes with the word on the left.

■ ASSEMBLY

Show the pupils the four words on the left-hand side of the screen by covering the words on the right with a piece of paper. Ask the pupils to read the words out and to say whether they think these are good words or bad words. Hopefully they will say that they are good words!

Let's look at the first word 'caring'. This is a good word. If someone said this about you they would be referring to a positive aspect of your character – we might call this a positive characteristic that you have. Now look at the four words next to the word 'caring'. Which word do you think goes best with the word 'caring'?

Listen to pupils' responses and discuss the meaning of the word *compassionate*.

Let's look at the second word 'sharing'. In maths if we are sharing we are dividing e.g. share six sweets between three people. How many do they have each? Accept the pupils' responses to this question.

Now think about the word 'sharing' in relation to an aspect of someone's character – if someone is a sharing person what type of person is she or he?

Now look at the other words on the left-hand side, finding the appropriate word on the right to match with each one. Allow plenty of discussion on each list, encouraging the pupils to understand the meanings of the words.

Which word is in every list? (selfish) Is this a good word or a bad word? It's a very common characteristic for any of us to have – we are all selfish at times. Of course, we think about our own needs and we think about the things that we want but we must always make sure that other people are not losing out because of us.

■ REFLECTION

When you have discussed all the lists, ask the pupils this question:

Are you a caring, compassionate, sharing, unselfish, smiling, laughing, friendly, considerate person? Try hard today to have all those characteristics. Let's all also try not to be selfish. Selfishness is a characteristic that we don't want to have. It's the opposite of a positive characteristic so we call it a negative characteristic.

Prayer

*Dear Lord,
Please help all of us to try hard to be caring, compassionate, sharing, smiling, laughing, friendly and considerate. Above all, help us not to be selfish.*

Amen

Song   Think, think on these things (Someone's Singing Lord, 38: *A&C Black*)

Positive characteristics

caring   mean   selfish   compassionate   unkind

sharing   dividing   unselfish   stealing   selfish

smiling   laughing   grimacing   selfish   scowling

friendly   selfish   inconsiderate   fighting   considerate

Team work

 **AIM: To encourage pupils to consider the wonder of the natural
world and to think about the importance of working together.**

> **PREPARATION**
> ■ Photocopy 'Team work' (page 10) ready to present on an OHP or through a
>   data projector.

■ INTRODUCTION

Begin by asking children how they would know if geese were flying overhead. Give the
children credit for coming up with answers such as 'they make a lot of noise' and 'they fly
in a v shape'.

■ ASSEMBLY

Show the picture of the geese on the OHP. Explain to pupils that there are very good
reasons for the noise that geese make and for the 'v' formation in which they fly.
Continue by telling pupils the following:

> *Geese need to cover very long distances when on their migratory path. The noise they
> make encourages the lead goose to keep going at a good pace, in the same way as you cheer
> people on Sports Day. Researchers have discovered that geese can fly about 70% further as
> a group than they can as individuals.*

> *The 'v' formation helps the geese to fly more easily because when each bird flaps its wings
> it causes uplift that creates less wind resistance for the bird behind. If a goose falls out of
> the formation it struggles to fly as quickly and easily. As the leading bird becomes tired,
> another bird will take a turn at the front to help keep them all flying along quickly.*

> *Sometimes a goose may become sick or injured and need to rest on the ground. When
> this happens, two other geese will go with it and stay until the injured or sick bird has
> recovered enough to continue its journey or cannot recover and has died. (Draw pupils'
> attention to the three geese on the stubble field.) When the birds on the ground are ready
> to continue their journey they wait for another group of geese to fly by and join them.*

> *When all the geese are ready to rest for the night they will often circle a suitable field
> several times 'honking' loudly. This not only ensures that they are landing in a safe place
> but also that any stragglers will see and hear where the rest of them are, so that every
> goose lands in the same safe area.*

■ REFLECTION

Ask pupils what we can learn from geese. Through their answers help them to understand
that we too need to encourage each other. We can achieve more when we work together
in a team. We should support those who, for whatever reason, find life difficult and help
them to become part of our team. We should accept new friends into our groups or
games just as geese accept new birds into their flocks and we should always try to
make sure that no 'stragglers' are left out.

Prayer

> *Dear Lord,*
> *Help us all to learn from the amazing things that geese can do because they work together
> as a group. Help us to encourage one another, to support those in difficulties, to take turns
> and to accept new friends into our groups. In this way we can all achieve more and make
> more of the lives you have given us.*
>
> *Amen*

Song

When I Needed a Neighbour (Someone's Singing Lord, 35: *A&C Black*)

Team work

Word chains

 AIM: To create a set of words, identifying which ones represent positive characteristics.

PREPARATION

■ This assembly should be presented after the assembly called 'Positive characteristics'.

■ Photocopy 'Word chains' (page 12) ready to present on an OHP.

■ Cover the list with a piece of paper so that you can reveal some of the words before others. You may also like to have marker pens so that you can add words.

INTRODUCTION

Remind the pupils of the last 'Positive characteristics' assembly, where they had to identify words from a list to match a word provided. Do they remember that all the words found were describing positive characteristics: caring, compassionate, sharing, unselfish, smiling, laughing, friendly, considerate? Do they remember the words that were describing negative characteristic: selfish and selfishness?

Today's words are linked and I will be asking you to try to spot how they are linked. Think about the title of today's assembly. It is called 'Word chains'.

ASSEMBLY

Show the pupils the first word on the list and discuss it. Chocolate may be considered a good word but is it a characteristic? Reveal the next word and discuss it. Keep revealing the words, one at a time, and discuss whether they describe positive characteristics. Once you have revealed all the words, ask the pupils to explain how the words are linked. (The answer is that the first letter of each word is the same as the final letter of the word before it.)

Which of the words describe positive characteristics?

Discuss the words 'wonderful', 'loving' and 'good' and how these words could describe positive aspects of people's characters.

Now, we are going to try a new word chain. I will give you a word. See if you can think of a word to follow it. Remember each new word has to start with the last letter of the word before it. If you can think of a word that follows this rule I will give you one point; but if you can think of a word that not only follows the rule but also represents a positive characteristic I will give you two points.

Start a new chain with the word 'garden', awarding points appropriately until no more new words can be added to the chain or until you decide that enough have been given. Now start with the word 'happiness' and again add words to the chain, awarding points to children who respond with sensible answers.

Ask any children who scored two points in either chain to stand up and to repeat their words for everyone to hear. Ensure that all the children understand that these words represent positive aspects of people's characters.

REFLECTION

How many positive descriptive words have we found? Those words represent characteristics that any one of us can have. Try to fit those descriptive words today. Try to show these positive characteristics today and maybe even to keep them beyond today.

Prayer

Dear Lord,
Please help all of us to try to be wonderful, loving, good, ... (add words that have been offered during the assembly).

Amen

Song   Think, think on these things (Someone's Singing Lord, 38: *A&C Black*)

Word chains

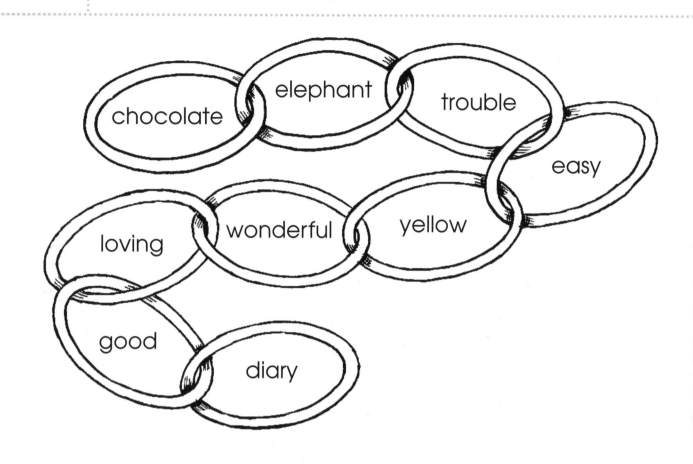

Andrew Brodie: Assembly Tomorrow KS2 © A&C Black Publishers Ltd. 2008

Dolphins

AIM: To encourage pupils to consider the wonder of the natural world and to learn from the behaviour of dolphins.

PREPARATION

■ Photocopy 'Dolphins' (page 14) on to an acetate sheet to display on the OHP.

▨ INTRODUCTION

Ask the children to identify the animal shown in the picture. Explain that the first part of today's activity is to complete a short quiz about dolphins. All the answers will be provided on the screen. The pupils simply have to pick the right answer to each question.

▨ ACTIVITY

How many different species of dolphin are there?

What is a male dolphin called?

What is a female dolphin called?

What is a baby dolphin called?

Dolphins live together in groups. What is the name for a group of dolphins?

Dolphins have a layer of fat under their skin, which helps to keep them warm. What is this called?

What do dolphins eat mainly?

What type of animals are dolphins?

Now let me tell you some other facts about dolphins.

- *Dolphins don't sleep like we do. They rest one side of their brain but keep one eye open, then they rest the other side and keep the other eye open.*

- *A dolphin breathes air like we do but it doesn't breathe through its nose. It has a blow hole in the top of its head and it has to come up to the surface of the water to breathe quite regularly.*

- *Dolphins live in groups called pods. There are usually about ten or twelve dolphins in a pod but sometimes lots of pods gather together to form a super pod.*

- *Dolphins can communicate by making sounds like clicks and whistles.*

- *Sometimes dolphins like to play with people who are swimming in the sea.*

▨ REFLECTION

Do you remember the assembly 'Team work' about geese and the way that geese help each other? One of the special things about dolphins is the way that they work together. Dolphins are members of pods and they support each other so that if one of them is ill or has been hurt, the others will stay with them and look after them. If we put our minds to it we can follow the example of the dolphins by working well together and helping each other.

Prayer

Dear God,
We thank you for the wonderful creatures of your world, as today we think about dolphins. Please help us to work together, supporting each other as dolphins do.
Amen

Song All things Bright and Beautiful (Come and Praise, 3: *BBC*)

Dolphins

bull

over 30

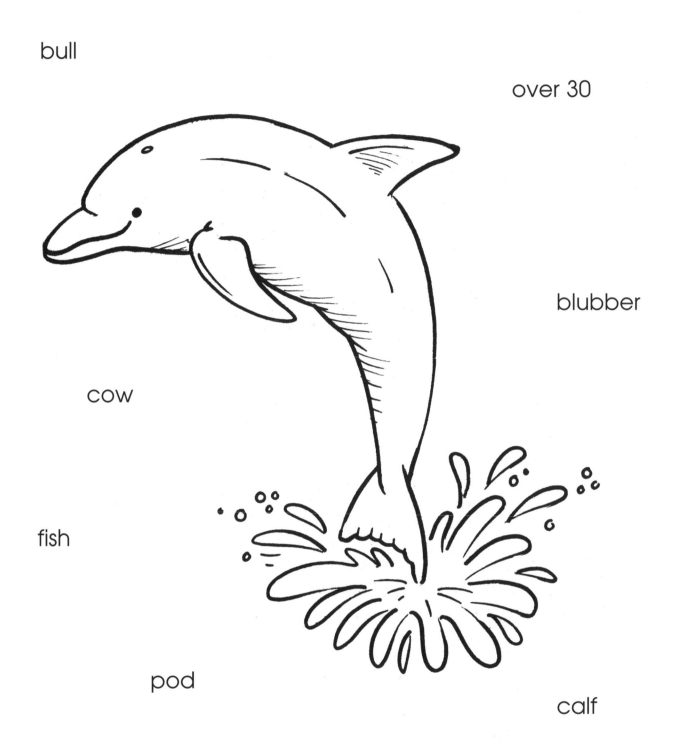

blubber

cow

fish

pod

calf

mammals

A prayer mat

 AIM: To understand that none of us can ever be perfect but that we can learn from our mistakes.

PREPARATION

■ Photocopy 'A prayer mat' (page 16) on to an acetate sheet to display on the OHP.

■ INTRODUCTION

Today we are going to look at a picture of a prayer mat and think about why these are important to the people who use them.

■ ASSEMBLY

Here is a picture of a prayer mat. Can any of you tell us the religion of the people who might use these? (Accept answer Islamic or Muslim).

Explain that Muslims may pray up to five times a day, placing their prayer mats on the ground to keep themselves clean. Being clean to pray is a sign of respect. Show pupils that the patterning on the mat is floral and geometric – there are no pictures of animals or humans. Mats are patterned in this way so that the person praying is not likely to be distracted from their prayers.

Ask the pupils to look very carefully at the prayer mat to see if they can spot anything that doesn't look quite right. (Someone should be able to tell you that there is a mistake in the patterning.)

Tell pupils that this mistake is very important, as it is a reminder that no human is perfect and that only God is perfect. Explain that we all make mistakes and that we probably forget just how often we make mistakes every day. Give them an example of a simple mistake you have made very recently e.g. mixing people's names up, perhaps calling somebody his brother's name or someone else her sister's name.

Ask pupils to think of a mistake they have made in the past. You could ask one or two volunteers to share their thoughts with everyone. Explain that we are all human and that we all make mistakes. The important thing is that we should try and learn from these mistakes.

■ REFLECTION

The prayer mat we have looked at is beautifully made, but has an error in it which reminds us that however clever we might be, no human being is perfect. We all make mistakes. Sometimes our mistake might affect somebody else. What should we do then?

Accept responses and encourage the children to realise that it is better to own up and say sorry than to try and avoid taking responsibility for the mistake.

Prayer

Dear Lord,
Help us to learn by the mistakes we make each day. Remind us that whilst we all have good brains that we use each day to learn new things, we don't get everything right all the time. Help us to accept the mistakes that our families and friends make each day and to encourage them to learn from these mistakes.

Amen

 Song Magic Penny (Alleluya, 10: *A&C Black*)

A prayer mat

 Andrew Brodie: Assembly Tomorrow KS2 © A&C Black Publishers Ltd. 2008

Charity

> **AIM: For pupils to understand the importance of using their time constructively and to appreciate the efforts of those who give their time to help others.**

PREPARATION
■ Photocopy 'Charity' (page 18) on to an acetate sheet and have a marker pen ready to add the names of charities to the sheet.

INTRODUCTION

Today we are going to think about charities, so firstly we need to be sure that we know what the word 'charity' means.

Show the title 'Charity' on the OHP. Ask pupils what they think the word 'charity' means. Accept all reasonable answers. Explain that there are several meanings listed in the dictionary including the definition that states charity involves giving to people in need.

For today's assembly we are going to think about charities as organisations that help others.

ASSEMBLY

Ask pupils to tell you of any charity that they know of e.g. NSPCC, RSPCA, Samaritans, Shelter, Children in Need, Comic Relief, etc. The list could include local charities as well as national charities. As the names of charities are suggested, write them on the acetate sheet.

Talk briefly about what each charity does. If you are unsure, you could suggest that groups of pupils research the work that a particular charity does, ready for a follow up assembly.

Explain to pupils that many of the people who work for these charities are volunteers. Ask them why they think people might volunteer to help with charity work. This can often include raising money to enable the work of the charity to continue, as well as working within the charity itself.

Do pupils think it is better to spend leisure time doing what they like or in finding ways to help others? Ask pupils to give reasons for their answers.

REFLECTION

It's important that we all understand that a lot of things that are done to help others are done through the work of charities. The people who give up their time to do charity work could spend their free time looking after themselves and enjoying their hobbies and pastimes, but they are very unselfish and are happy to work for others. All religions ask people to care about and help one another. We should all be grateful to the people who spend their free time doing this.

Prayer

Dear Lord,
We give thanks for the people who care enough to give up their time to help others – those involved with keeping children and animals safe and secure; those who give food and shelter to those who would otherwise have none; and those who reach out to others regardless of their race or beliefs.

Amen

Song   Make me a channel of your peace (Alleluya, 43: *A&C Black*)

CHARITIES WE KNOW

Christmas preparations

 AIM: To help pupils consider the true meaning of Christmas.

PREPARATION

- Photocopy 'Christmas preparations' (page 20) ready for display on the OHP. You could also have a child or a group of children primed to read the poem to the assembly.

INTRODUCTION

Show the poem and either read it to, or with, the children. Alternatively, you could cover the poem and have an individual or small group of pupils recite it.

ASSEMBLY

Ask pupils who the 'I' in the poem refers to. (Hopefully they will realise that it is Jesus Christ.)

Discuss the meaning of the poem with the pupils and find out from them why they think Christmas is celebrated. Ask how many of them have a religious aspect to their Christmas celebrations e.g. how many might go to church during the Christmas period?

Draw the pupils' attention to the illustrations with the poem and point out that there is no religious aspect to these. Ask them to suggest how the poem could have been illustrated differently to help people to think about the real meaning of Christmas.

REFLECTION

Encourage pupils to think about how they could enhance their Christmas celebrations in more meaningful and less commercial ways. Help them to realise that the way they behave towards one another is more important than any gifts they receive or give.

Of course it's nice to receive presents but it's very nice to give presents too, just to see the look on the face of the person who is receiving them. As well as presents, we need to think about the true meaning of Christmas – the birth of Jesus and all that he taught us about unselfishness and helpfulness towards other people.

Prayer

Dear Jesus,
Please help us all to remember the true meaning of Christmas. If we think about the celebration of your birth on earth we will also think about how you would like us to live. Help us to remember the needs of others before ourselves as we enjoy this festive time.

Song   A starry night (Merrily to Bethlehem, 7: *A&C Black*)

Christmas Preparations

Advent is now upon us
So here we go again,
With calendars and candles,
Each year it feels the same.

The shops are full of twinkling lights,
Of Santas, and of elves.
Everybody Christmas shopping,
Thinking mainly of themselves.

I'd like to be included
In this festive time of joy,
To be thought of by the children
As they unwrap each new toy.

It's time for Christmas dinner,
Full of happiness and fun.
I wish that I could be there
But they haven't said, "Please come."

Each year they sing about me.
I often hear my name, but
They've forgotten to invite me,
To celebrate my reign.

When Christmas time is over,
And decorations packed away.
Though they haven't thought about me,
For your sake I'm here to stay.

Andrew Brodie: Assembly Tomorrow KS2 © A&C Black Publishers Ltd. 2008

Angels

 AIM: To look at the role of angels in the Christmas story.

PREPARATION

■ Photocopy 'Angels' (page 22) ready to present on an OHP.

■ INTRODUCTION

Begin by showing the picture upside down or sideways and ask pupils what they think the picture shows. Turn it the correct way up and ask if it's now easier to see what it is. Someone will see the shape and tell you that it's an angel. Ask how they know this. Hopefully they will mention the shape of the wings and the pose.

■ ASSEMBLY

Ask pupils what they think angels do. Accept all reasonable answers and use them to help everyone understand that angels are said to be messengers of God who guide people towards the correct actions. They may warn of danger or help guide people along a path in life. Angels are mentioned in both Christian and Jewish stories.

Ask pupils what they know about the role of angels in the Christmas story. Answers should include: Mary being visited by an angel to be told that she was to have a baby; Joseph being told by an angel of the baby; the shepherds seeing the 'heavenly host' announcing the birth; and the wise men being warned by an angel not to tell Herod of the whereabouts of the baby. Someone may even volunteer the fact that the Bible says that after the death of Herod, by which time Mary, Joseph and Jesus were in Egypt, an angel visited Joseph to say that it was safe to return to Israel.

■ REFLECTION

Visits by angels occur in many places in the Bible. They play quite an important role in the story of the birth of Jesus. We imagine that an angel may look rather like the 'Christmas Angel' picture we are looking at today, but in fact no one really knows what an angel may have looked like or even if they appeared in different ways to different people. However, what's important is not what they looked like, but that they helped people to do what God wanted.

We often refer to angels in our everyday speech. Someone might say, 'Be an angel and dry the dishes', or 'Sophie was a real angel today because she worked so hard and she helped other people'. Sometimes nurses who work in hospitals are given the nickname 'angels'. Why do you think they have this nickname?

Leave the pupils with this thought: *I wonder if angels exist in the world today? Many people believe they do. What do you think?*

Explain that you have just given them this to think about, not to actually answer.

Prayer

Dear Lord,
Thank you for the angels that you have sent to help people to live their lives well and safely. Thank you for the people who act as angels in our lives, those who help us to do the right things, to keep us safe and well, and guide us on the correct paths through life.
Amen

Song Gabriel's message (Merrily to Bethlehem, 2: *A&C Black*)

Angels

Andrew Brodie: Assembly Tomorrow KS2 © A&C Black Publishers Ltd. 2008

The right beliefs

AIM: To respect the beliefs of others.

PREPARATION

■ Photocopy 'The right beliefs' (page 24) on to an acetate sheet.

▨ INTRODUCTION

*Sadly, many arguments are caused by peoples' inability to try to understand the
religious ideas of others. Today we have a story to help us to think about this problem.*
(Show the picture.)

▨ STORY

*A group of young people were just beginning to enjoy a day out at a local museum when it
dawned upon them that they were members of several different religions. In the group there
was a Christian, a Jew, a Muslim and a Sikh. They began to argue about their faiths, each
believing that what they believed and the way they worshipped was the only correct way.
This argument, between students who were usually very good friends, became more and
more heated. The friends' voices were getting louder and louder as they each tried to tell
the others about how their beliefs were right and how the others were completely wrong.*

*Their teacher, hearing the noise, went across to them to see what the problem was. He
took the students into a rather damp courtyard outside the museum and asked each of them
what they had seen inside the museum in the short time they had been there. The first one
said that he had seen a large model of a dinosaur, the second said she had noticed the
museum had a shop to buy gifts, the third had looked at some very old paintings and
the fourth had noticed the display of old bottles, cups and dishes.*

*Before they got too wet outside, their teacher asked them all if they had been in the same
place, and if they had all been protected from the weather in the warm dry museum and
if any of them had any reason not to believe what each of the others had seen in there.
He told them that if they thought carefully about this, they would find the answer to their
earlier argument.*

*The four young people went into the dry and thought carefully about what had been said.
They soon understood that they had indeed found the answer to their argument.
Have you?*

▨ REFLECTION

See if pupils can explain the story, and more importantly its resolution, to you. They
should realise that we all might, through religious beliefs, see things in different ways,
just as the students noticed different things in the museum. In fact, we are living in the
same world and we are all looking for the protection and guidance of a God, just as the
building protected the students from the weather.

Prayer

*Dear Lord,
Help us all to live together in peace and to respect each other's ideas; please help others to
understand ours. Help us all to shine a light of understanding on the beliefs and ways of
life of all those around us.*

Amen

Song   This little light of mine (Alleluya, 14: *A&C Black*)

The right beliefs

The creation story

 AIM: To help pupils to understand the Christian creation story.

PREPARATION

- Photocopy 'The creation story' (page 26) on to an acetate sheet.
- If using an OHP you could cover each of the pictures with a circle of plain dark paper so that you can reveal the pictures one at a time or you could cut out the pictures first and then add them gradually to the presentation.

INTRODUCTION

For many thousands of years, people in all parts of the world have told stories that attempt to explain how the world was made and how people came into existence. Today we are going to look at the Christian creation story.

ACTIVITY

At the very beginning of time there was nothing – no earth, no sun, no moon, no stars – absolutely nothing. God began the work of creation by making light. (Show the first picture.) *He separated light from dark, calling the light 'day' and the dark 'night'.*

Next he made the earth and the sky. He made the earth into areas of water and areas of dry land. (Show second picture.) *However, there was still no life on this new world so God made grass, trees, flowers and all the plants.* (Show the third picture.)

He was pleased with what had been done but knew that his job was not yet complete. In the skies God placed the moon, sun and many stars. (Show the fourth picture.) *There was still more work to do so God made all kinds of fish to live in the seas and birds to fly in the air.* (Show the fifth picture.)

Nearing the end of his wonderful work of creation, God made all the different kinds of animals that walk, run and jump on the earth. Finally God made his greatest creation, humans. (Show the sixth picture.)

With his work completed in just six days, God looked at what he had done and was pleased, so on the seventh day he rested. He made this final day a special day, a day of rest for all people.

Even today, one day each week is considered special; a day for rest, for worship and for family. What day of the week is this?

Explain that in the Christian religion the day of rest is Sunday when most people do not go to work. You could elaborate on this by explaining that only a few years ago there were no shops open on Sunday and very few people worked, but now lots of people go shopping on Sunday and many people do have to work.

REFLECTION

Even though scientists now have other theories about how life on earth developed, over not seven days but millions of years, this story helps us to think about the amazing world in which we live. We have huge oceans and vast areas of land; we have grass, trees, flowers, animals and birds; we have the sun we can see in the daytime and the moon and stars we can see at night.

Prayer
*Dear Lord,
Help us to care for this precious world you made for us. We thank you for the day and night, the water and land, the plants, the animals and all other humans.*

Amen

Song The building song (Alleluya, 59: *A&C Black*)

The creation story

Joseph (Part 1)

 AIM: To learn about one of the most famous Bible stories.

PREPARATION

■ Photocopy 'Joseph (Part 1)' (page 28) on to an acetate sheet ready to show on the OHP – you may like to ask some older pupils to colour it carefully before you use it.

■ **INTRODUCTION**

Today's story is one of the stories from Genesis, one of the 'books' in the Bible. As it is a long story, it will take three assemblies to tell the whole story. Can you guess the name of the person the story is about? I'll show you a picture of him in his coat.

■ **STORY**

The story is about a young man called Joseph whose father was called Jacob. Joseph had eleven brothers: Reuben, Simeon, Levi, Judah, Issachar, Zebulun, Dan, Naphtali, Gad, Asher and Benjamin. Because Joseph was Jacob's favourite son, he made him a special coat to wear. Joseph's brothers were very jealous. "Why did Father make him a smart coat and not us?" they said.

To make matters worse, Joseph told his brothers about his dreams. "One night I dreamt that we were on the farm tying up bundles of wheat. My bundle of wheat was standing straight and tall and your bundles bowed down to it." He went on to say, "Last night I had another dream. The sun and the moon and eleven stars in the sky all bowed down to me."

Who do you think the eleven stars could represent? Who do you think the sun and moon could represent? Ensure that they understand that the eleven stars represent the brothers and the sun and moon represent Joseph's parents.

Why do you think Joseph's brothers hated him? Establish that they were jealous but they were also cross with Joseph for suggesting that they should bow down to him.

One day the brothers were out in the fields looking after the sheep and goats. Jacob sent Joseph to find out if everything was all right. When the brothers saw Joseph coming they decided to kill him, to throw his body into a well, then to tell their father that a wild animal had killed him. The oldest brother, Reuben, said they shouldn't kill him but should just throw him into the well. So that's exactly what they did, after tearing off his special coat.

The brothers sat down to eat their lunch. As they sat there, they noticed a group of traders travelling with their camels who were loaded with spices to be sold in Egypt.

"Let's sell Joseph to the traders," said Judah. So they pulled Joseph up from the well and sold him for twenty pieces of silver.

After Joseph had gone, the brothers killed one of the goats and put blood on his special coat. They took the coat and returned home to Jacob. When he saw the blood-stained coat he assumed that a wild animal had killed Joseph. He was grief-stricken.

■ **REFLECTION**

Discuss the following questions with the children, encouraging them to express their points of view:

Do you think that Joseph was unkind to his brothers? Do you think that the brothers were unkind to Joseph? Were they right to be jealous? Were they right to sell him?

Prayer

Dear God,
Please help us not to show off to other people because we can upset them and make them jealous. Please help us not to be jealous of other people ourselves and help us not to be unkind to other people.

Amen

Song   The Journey of Life (Someone's Singing Lord, 28: *A&C Black*)

Joseph (Part 1)

Joseph (Part 2)

 AIM: To learn about one of the most famous Bible stories.

PREPARATION

■ Photocopy 'Joseph (Part 2)' (page 30) on to an acetate sheet ready to show on the OHP.

INTRODUCTION

Remind the pupils of the previous assembly about Joseph by asking them questions such as: Do they remember which book of the Bible the story is from? Do they remember how many brothers Joseph had? Do they remember why the brothers were jealous of Joseph? Do they remember his father's name? Explain that today's story continues from the last assembly and is the second part of the Joseph story.

STORY

The traders who bought Joseph took him to Egypt and sold him as a slave to a man called Potiphar. Joseph worked hard for Potiphar and, because he was clever and a hard worker, he was made chief servant. Potiphar's wife, however, decided to get Joseph into trouble. She accused him of all sorts of things that he hadn't done. He was sent to prison.

In prison Joseph met two other prisoners. They were two of the king's most important servants, his butler and his baker, but because they had upset the king he had put them in prison. One night the butler and the baker each had a dream and they told Joseph all about them. The butler's dream was about a grapevine with three branches and in the dream the butler squeezed the juice from the grapes into the king's cup. Joseph explained what the dream meant. He said that in three days time the king would release the butler and give him his old job back. Joseph explained the baker's dream too and three days later both of Joseph's explanations came true.

Two more years passed by and then the king started having dreams himself. In one of them he dreamt that he saw seven fat cows come out of the River Nile followed by seven thin cows. The thin cows ate the fat cows. The king was very worried about his dreams and he told his butler all about them. The butler suggested that Joseph might help.

The king sent for Joseph and told him about the dreams. Joseph was able to explain them straight away. "There will be seven years of good harvests and lots of food, then there will be seven years of poor harvests and famine," he said. "You need to put a man in charge of the harvests for the next fourteen years to make sure that some corn is kept from the seven good years ready for the seven bad years. You will need lots of big barns to store the corn and you will need to guard it well."

The king decided that the best person to put in charge was Joseph. So Joseph, who had been a slave and a prisoner, suddenly became one of the most important people in Egypt.

REFLECTION

Was it fair that Joseph was sent to prison? Why was Joseph the best person to put in charge for the fourteen years?

Encourage the children to appreciate that he was the one with a plan – he had used his brain to think of a solution to the problem.

 Prayer

Dear God,
Please help us to use our brains to solve problems. We are lucky to be able to think so many thoughts – help us to make good use of our thinking power to deal with the problems that face us every day.

Amen

 Song

The Journey of Life (Someone's Singing Lord, 28: *A&C Black*)

Joseph (Part 2)

Joseph (Part 3)

 AIM: To learn about one of the most famous Bible stories.

PREPARATION

■ Photocopy the 'Joseph (Part 3)' (page 32) on to an acetate sheet ready to show on the OHP.

INTRODUCTION

Remind the pupils of the previous assembly about Joseph by asking them questions. Can they remember the king's dreams? Do they remember Joseph's plan? Explain that today's story continues from the last assembly and is the third part of the Joseph story.

STORY

Just as Joseph had predicted, the seven years of famine came and many countries were very short of food. So Joseph opened his barns and began to sell the corn to the people of Egypt.

Back in the land of Canaan, where Joseph's brothers lived with their father, the famine was very bad. Jacob heard that there was corn for sale in Egypt so he sent ten of his sons (not including Benjamin, the youngest son) to buy food. They didn't recognise Joseph and they bowed down to him. Joseph didn't tell them who he was. He wanted to know if they were sorry for what they had done to him so many years ago.

"You are spies from another country," he said and he threw them into prison. Then he told them he would let them go if they brought their youngest brother to see him. Joseph kept one of the brothers as a prisoner and sent the others away with full sacks of corn. He also put all their money back in with the corn so that they could take that back home too.

When they got home they told Jacob all about what had happened to them. "You cannot take Benjamin," he said. "He is my youngest son and I have already lost Joseph."

So the brothers stayed in Canaan until all the corn was used up and everyone was hungry again. Reluctantly, Jacob agreed to let them go back to Egypt with Benjamin.

When they got to Egypt, Joseph provided a great feast and he arranged the table so that the brothers sat in age order. The brothers were amazed that he knew the order of these ages.

The next day the eleven brothers set off home. Joseph had arranged for their sacks to be filled with corn and their money. However, in Benjamin's sack he hid his own silver cup.

Not long after his brothers had left, Joseph sent his servant to catch up with them, claiming his cup had been taken. The servant brought the brothers back and Joseph told them that whoever had the cup would become his slave. The cup was found in Benjamin's sack. Judah begged for Benjamin to be allowed to go home and that he would stay instead.

Because Judah was willing to sacrifice himself to save Benjamin, Joseph knew that his brothers were sorry for what they had done and he told them who he was. "Go back and fetch my father and all the other members of the family," Joseph told them. "You can all come and live here." So Jacob's whole family moved to Egypt and that is how the Israelites settled in Egypt.

REFLECTION

Was it fair that Joseph tricked his brothers? What story tells us how the Israelites left Egypt many, many years later?

Prayer

Dear God,
Please help us to value our families: our brothers and sisters; our parents; our uncles and aunts; our cousins; our grandparents.

Amen

Song   The Journey of Life (Someone's Singing Lord 28: *A&C Black*)

Joseph (Part 3)

Andrew Brodie: Assembly Tomorrow KS2 © A&C Black Publishers Ltd. 2008

Escape from Egypt

AIM: To appreciate the role that trust plays in life.

PREPARATION

■ Photocopy 'Escape from Egypt' (page 34) on to an acetate sheet ready to present on the OHP.

■ Choose some confident older pupils who can practise the poem before the assembly, so that they can present it to the others. They will need to pick up on the rhythm of the poem and may like to present it as a rap.

INTRODUCTION

You may decide to begin by asking the children what they know about the story of Moses and the escape from Egypt. (The story can be found in *Assembly Today for Key Stage 2*.) Use any contribution the pupils make to discuss this story with them. Emphasise how brave the Israelites must have been to place their trust in a God whom they could not see or talk to directly. Ask the pupils how the Israelites came to be living in Egypt in the first place. Hopefully they will remember the story of Joseph that they have heard in the three previous assemblies.

Explain to the children that Joseph brought the Israelites to live in Egypt and that they lived very happily with the Egyptians for a very long time but eventually there were disputes between the two groups. At that point, Moses led the Israelites in their escape from Egypt.

ASSEMBLY

Show the poem and read it through with the children or ask the older pupils who have practised it to read it out. Ask the children why they think the last verse is only two lines long, though the other verses each have ten lines. They should be able to tell you that the final verse only needs two lines to sum up the idea that the whole of the story can be thought of as a message. The message is about the importance of placing trust in God in difficult situations.

REFLECTION

There are times in our lives when we have to put our trust in others just as Moses put his trust in God. Even then it wasn't easy for the Israelites to leave Egypt and find freedom.

rayer

Dear Lord,
Help us to learn when to place our trust in others to help us through difficult situations in our lives. Help us to understand that often problems that seem impossible to deal with can be sorted out when we place our trust in you.

Amen

ong   I'm on my way (Alleluya, 27: *A&C Black*)

Escape from Egypt

Moses went to the Pharaoh, feeling very brave,
He said, " You shouldn't use the Israelites to be your slaves.
They work and they toil in the midday sun,
Pharaoh, oh Pharaoh, this just shouldn't be done."
Pharaoh gave a chuckle, he thought it was a joke,
"Now, now Moses, you're a good bloke.
There are wells to be dug and holes to be filled,
Fields to be tended and pyramids to build.
People need to work hard on all the building sites,
So why shouldn't it be the Israelites?"

Moses prayed to God: " Help us out of this mess,
I know that you'll take care of us, you always know what's best."
So God sent down, to annoy the Egyptians,
A series of disasters and dreadful afflictions.
A river of blood, then frogs, then gnats,
Flies, dead animals and hail that ruined flax,
After locusts and darkness still Pharaoh he said, "No!"
But when the firstborn were killed, the Egyptians said, " Go!"
At last, thought Moses, my people can be led
Away from this land full of misery and dread.

The Israelites felt happy, getting ready to leave,
But old Pharaoh still had one more trick, tucked up his sleeve.
He sent out his army to catch every one
And kill them as they made their way away in the sun.
As the Israelites started, to leave his land,
Led by a cloud through a desert of sand,
They saw what was happening and started to flee
But found themselves trapped at the edge of the sea.
The waters they parted and the Israelites fled,
Then it covered the Egyptians and drowned them, dead!

This tale has a message for me and for you.
Put your trust in God and he will always help you through.

Andrew Brodie: Assembly Tomorrow KS2 © A&C Black Publishers Ltd. 2008

The Ten Commandments

AIM: To learn about the Ten Commandments.

PREPARATION

■ Photocopy the Ten Commandments (page 36) on to an acetate sheet ready to present on the OHP.

■ You could link this assembly to the assembly about the Native Americans Commandments (pages 37 and 38).

INTRODUCTION

Remind the pupils of the story of Moses leading the Israelites out of Egypt. The story is included in *Assembly Today for Key Stage 2* and is also summarised in the poem on page 34 of this book.

The Bible tells us that the Israelites lived in the desert for forty years, eating food called manna and drinking water that sprang from a rock. Moses led the people to a mountain called Mount Sinai. He climbed the mountain with his brother Aaron and while they were there, God told them the rules that the people should follow. These rules are called the Ten Commandments.

ASSEMBLY

Show the pupils the first commandment on the OHP screen. Discuss each one in turn, showing sensitivity to the needs of the pupils in your school. You may wish to talk pupils through the commandments quite quickly, concentrating on the last three as they are perhaps most relevant to the children's lives.

REFLECTION

Discuss the fact that all societies and all communities need to have rules to follow. The Bible tells us that God gave these commandments for his people to follow. You could discuss the fact that your school has rules for everyone to follow, asking the pupils why the rules are there. Hopefully they will be able to explain that the rules are there for the benefit everybody – some may be for safety, some may be related to good manners and some may be concerned with other aspects of relationships with other people.

rayer

Dear Lord,
Help us to follow the rules that exist in our school to help us to lead peaceful lives and to help others to be happy too. Help us to think about the rules that we have looked at today and to consider how they may be useful in our own lives.

Amen

ong

Think, think on these things (Someone's Singing Lord, 38: *A&C Black*)

The Ten Commandments

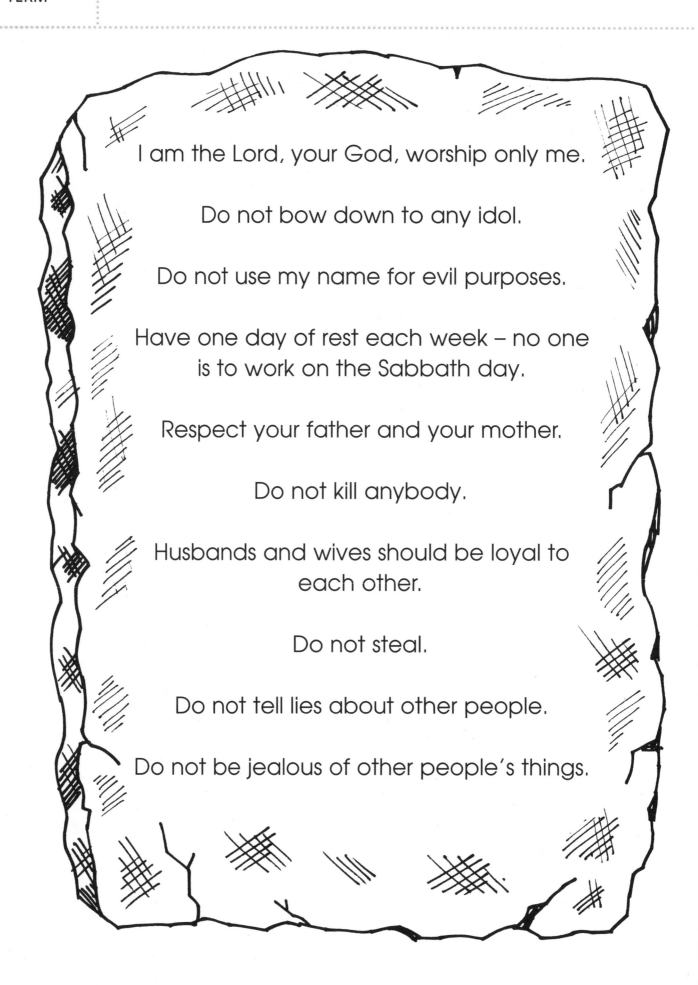

I am the Lord, your God, worship only me.

Do not bow down to any idol.

Do not use my name for evil purposes.

Have one day of rest each week – no one
is to work on the Sabbath day.

Respect your father and your mother.

Do not kill anybody.

Husbands and wives should be loyal to
each other.

Do not steal.

Do not tell lies about other people.

Do not be jealous of other people's things.

Andrew Brodie: Assembly Tomorrow KS2 © A&C Black Publishers Ltd. 2008

Native American Indian Commandments

AIM: To understand that we all need rules to live by.

PREPARATION

■ Photocopy 'Native American Indian Commandments' (page 38) ready to present on the OHP.

■ INTRODUCTION

Remind the children that all communities need rules to live by. Rules enable everyone to co-exist peacefully together. Remind them of the assembly in which you introduced the Ten Commandments. Do they remember where the Ten Commandments came from? Can they remember any of them? Ask pupils to tell you some of the rules in school that help everyone to function safely and happily. Accept all appropriate answers.

■ ASSEMBLY

Explain that many years ago, in North America, the tribes of people who lived there abided by a set of rules. There were different tribes who spoke different languages and had different ways of life, but they all understood the importance of following the rules of life. These people particularly understood how important it was to look after the land around them and to keep it safe for future generations.

Here is one version of the rules that some of the Native American people followed in their daily lives. We are going to look at them together and make sure we understand them. (Show the Commandments).

Talk about each of the Commandments with the pupils, explaining what each of them means. Ensure pupils understand that the 'Great Spirit' is a higher being – one that many people would call 'God'. Then ask pupils if they think that these are a good set of rules for life.

■ REFLECTION

The Native Americans understood the need for rules to live by and these included the very important idea of caring for the world around them and never taking more from the land than they needed to live on. Encourage the children to realise that these Commandments, like the Ten Commandments in the Bible, are there to guide us in our thinking. We should think carefully about each one to see if they help us in the way that we live our lives.

Prayer

Dear Lord,
Help us to follow the rules that are there to help us to lead peaceful lives and to help others to be happy too. Help us to think about the rules that we have looked at today and to consider how they may be useful in our own lives.

Amen

Song

Peace is flowing like a river (Alleluya, 48: *BBC*)

Native American Indian Commandments

The Earth is your mother; care for her.

Open your heart and soul to the Great Spirit.

Give thanks to the Great Spirit for each new day.

Honour all of your relatives.

All life is sacred; treat all beings with respect.

Do what needs to be done for the good of all.

Speak the truth but only for the good of others.

Take from the Earth what is needed and nothing more.

Follow the rhythms of nature.

Enjoy life's journey but leave no tracks.

Andrew Brodie: Assembly Tomorrow KS2 © A&C Black Publishers Ltd. 2008

Day and Night

 AIM: To appreciate the daily cycle of darkness and light.

PREPARATION

■ Photocopy 'Day and Night' (page 40) ready to present on an OHP. Reveal each part of the picture as that point in the story is reached.

■ INTRODUCTION

Remind the children of the assembly about the Christian creation story from the Book of Genesis in the Bible. Explain that throughout the world different faiths and cultures have stories about how the world was made and that this morning they will be learning about a creation myth told by the Cherokee Indian tribe called 'The Legend of the Cedar Tree'.

■ STORY

In the very earliest of days, when the first people lived on the earth, they were dismayed when each bright new day was followed by a dark cold night. It would, they thought, be so much better if it was light all the time. The maker of the world heard them and decided to grant their wish. From that moment, there was no more darkness. The plant life grew unceasingly and very soon it was difficult to walk through the woodlands, which were overgrown with bushes and nettles.

After a few weeks the people struggled with this permanent sunlight and as they were finding it difficult to sleep, they became more and more irritable. They realised that their longing for permanent daylight had been wrong and thought instead that it would be far better to have night all the time. Again, the creator of the world decided to keep the people happy by granting their wishes, though he felt it was not the natural way of the world that he had intended.

From that moment on, the daylight faded into darkness and the velvety blackness of night filled the world. For a few hours the people enjoyed the refreshingly cool air, but very soon they began to collect firewood to light fires. It was, of course, difficult to search for wood in the dark, and difficult to hunt for food in the constant blackness. The result of this was that some of the people died from the cold and others died from starvation.

The people soon regretted their request for darkness and once again turned to the creator. This time they asked for the world to be changed back to the pattern of day following night the way it did before. The creator again listened to the people and realised that they had learned that their previous requests had been foolish. From then on, day followed night in the proper way and the people were happy.

The creator was sad about those who had died and so he created a reminder of how perfectly he had made the world and how unnecessary it was to change anything. To do this he created a brand new tree, the cedar tree. In the wood of each cedar tree he placed the spirit of one of the tribe's ancestors. This tree was considered special and to this day pieces of the tree bark are placed near doorways to prevent evil spirits entering Cherokee homes.

■ REFLECTION

Ask pupils to think about how it would affect their lives if we had all daylight or all darkness. Would there be any advantages to either of these situations? What would the problems be?

Prayer

Dear Lord,
We thank you for the cycles that occur in our lives – of day and night, dark and light,
seasons of the year and the weather that we have during each of them.

Amen

Song   I danced in the morning (Someone's Singing Lord, 29: *A&C Black*)

Day and night

Andrew Brodie: Assembly Tomorrow KS2 © A&C Black Publishers Ltd. 2008

Our world in space

AIM: To help pupils wonder at the magnitude of space.

PREPARATION

■ Photocopy 'Our world in space' (page 42) on to acetate ready for display on the OHP.

■ INTRODUCTION

Ask the pupils if they have ever looked into the night sky and tried counting the stars.

Today we are going to think about ourselves, our world and our place in space.

■ ACTIVITY

Begin by asking questions and accepting answers about space such as:

What is a planet?
What is the solar system?
What are stars?
What is a galaxy?
What is the Milky Way?

After the inevitable answers relating to chocolate bars, discuss the fact that the chocolate bars have been named after these space terms! 'Mars' is a planet; a galaxy is a system of stars all connected together by gravity. The 'Milky Way' is a band of light that can be seen across the sky at night and consisting of millions of distant stars. The solar system is the collection of planets, of which our earth is one, that travel around the sun.

You may decide to ask other factual questions as well. Your final question should be:

Do you think there is life on other worlds?

Ask for a show of hands for positive and negative responses then ask for reasons for these opinions. Explain that for many years, people have made up stories about space travel and wondered about life existing on far away planets. Space rockets have visited some of the planets and some very special rockets have been to the moon but no one have ever been to any of the stars or planets outside our solar system.

■ REFLECTION

Sometimes we call the sky above us when it's full of stars 'the heavens' and we call the sun, the moon, the planets and the stars 'heavenly bodies'. Perhaps it's because when we look up at the millions of stars in the sky it seems like heaven.

It is amazing to think that our planet has developed in such a way as to give us all life. However, many people believe that life began on our planet and that life is very rare and therefore precious. We know that there are many planets that have no life on them and no one knows yet if there is life on more distant worlds. Perhaps one day we will discover other planets that can support life, but no one can be sure of that. With the privilege of life on this wonderful planet it is important that we take care of it, for ourselves, for other creatures and for the future.

Prayer

Dear Lord,
We thank you for the richness of life on our amazing planet. For day and night, for land and water, for fish, birds, animals and plants. Help us to remember each day what a miracle it is that this planet supports such a diversity of life.

Amen

Song

I watch the sunrise (Alleluya, 15: *A&C Black*)

Our world in space

Seasons

AIM: To consider the seasons of the year.

> **PREPARATION**
> ■ Photocopy 'Seasons 1' (page 44) and 'Seasons 2' (page 45) on to acetate sheets for display on the OHP.

▨ INTRODUCTION

Ask the children if they know what season it is now. Discuss the season and what the weather is like. Discuss the fact that at the moment we have nice long evenings when it stays light and we can go outside. Can the children remember any features of the other seasons? Can they remember the dark evenings of the winter and the cold weather?

▨ ASSEMBLY

Turn on the OHP to show the seasons wheel with summer at the top.

Look at the seasons wheel. It's now the summer time. The months of June, July and August are in the summer.

Turn the sheet to put autumn at the top.

After the summer we have the autumn when the leaves turn brown and fall off the trees; the weather gets colder and we often have windy weather. The months of September, October and November are in the autumn. Can anybody think of any special events that take place in the autumn time?

Accept contributions, which may include events such as Harvest Festival, Halloween and Bonfire Night.

Turn the sheet to put winter at the top.

After the autumn we get to winter when the weather is cold and it goes dark very early, not long after we get home from school. The months of December, January and February are in the winter. Can anybody think of any special events that take place in the winter time?

Accept contributions, which may include events such as Christmas and New Year.

Turn the sheet to put spring at the top.

Spring comes next and the weather begins to get warm again. The months of March, April and May are in spring. Can anybody think of any special events that take place in the spring time?

Accept contributions, which may include events such as Easter and May Day.

Turn the sheet to get back to summer at the top.

Then we get back to the summer. Which season do you like best?

▨ REFLECTION

Encourage the children to think about the current season and emphasise its good features. As an extension activity you could ask the children how many days are in each month and teach them the traditional rhyme as shown on page 45.

'rayer

Dear Lord,
Thank you for the changing seasons. We thank you for the summer weather and the lovely long evenings. We thank you for the colourful leaves in the autumn, the snow in the winter and the flowers in the spring. We thank you for every month and the changes each month brings. Help us to enjoy every day of every month throughout the year.

Amen

ong To God who makes all lovely things (Someone's Singing Lord, 9: *A&C Black*)

Seasons 1

Thirty days has September,
April, June and November.
All the rest have thirty-one,
Except for February alone,
Which has twenty-eight days clear
And twenty-nine in each leap year.

Rumours

 AIM: To encourage children to avoid spreading rumours and telling untrue tales.

PREPARATION

■ Photocopy 'Rumours' (page 47) on to an acetate sheet ready to present on the OHP.

▨ INTRODUCTION

Today's story is adapted from a very old story from India. It comes from the Kathasaritsagara (which means the Ocean of Streams of Stories) and was written by Somadeva in the eleventh century.

▨ STORY

In the city of Kusumapura near the River Ganges in India lived a man named Harasvamin. He was a very good man and, because of this, another man became jealous of him.

"Do you know Harasvamin?" the unkind man said. "Do you know what he does? He eats children."
"Yes, I know," agreed another unkind person, even though it was not true at all.
"I've heard that too," added somebody else.

And so the unkind story was passed on from person to person. Of course, it was the unkind people who had started the rumour but other people began to listen and soon lots of people believed it was true. They started to keep their children indoors in case poor old Harasvamin ate them.

After a while, the people decided that Harasvamin should leave the city. They sent some messengers to tell him to leave. "You must leave this city!" they called to him from a distance – they didn't want to get too close because they thought he was too dangerous.

Harasvamin was completely taken by surprise. "Why do you want me to leave?" he asked. "Because you are eating children!" the messengers replied.

Harasvamin decided he would speak to the people who had sent the messengers. "Do you know of any children that I have eaten?" he asked. "Has anybody lost a child?"

The people turned to each other and asked which children had disappeared and which children had been eaten. Of course, nobody could name any children that had disappeared or had been eaten and they realised that they had been listening to a false rumour. "We are very sorry," they said to Harasvamin.

Despite the apology and even though people begged him to stay, Harasvamin decided he didn't want to stay in a city where people had spread nasty rumours about him.

▨ REFLECTION

Do you ever tell tales about other people that are not true? The story of Harasvamin shows us that we should be very careful about what we say. We can hurt other people by spreading rumours. Telling untrue tales is a type of bullying and we don't want any bullying in this school or in our lives at all. Of course, there are times when we must tell our teacher or our parents about something that is worrying us and that is fine if we are telling the truth.

Prayer

Dear Lord,
Please help us not to tell tales and not to believe nasty rumours. Help us to be very careful with what we say and also to be very careful with what we hear. Help us to always tell the truth.

Amen

 Song

The ink is black, the page is white (Someone's Singing Lord, 39: *A&C Black*)

Occupations

AIM: To consider the huge variety of occupations and the skills needed for these.

PREPARATION
■ Photocopy 'Occupations' (page 49) on to an acetate sheet to show on the OHP. Have a spare acetate sheet and some marker pens available.

▦ INTRODUCTION

Tell the children that today they will be thinking about occupations. Explain that an occupation is another word for a job.

We might say to someone, 'what is your occupation?' and we mean, 'what is your job?'

Can you think of another word that means something similar to occupation or job? We might say to someone, 'how are you employed?' or 'what is your employment?'

Turn on the OHP and ask the pupils to explain each of the occupations shown.

▦ ASSEMBLY

Ask the pupils to think quietly for a short while. Explain that you are going to make a list of occupations and they should try to think of occupations to add to the list. They could think of their own parents' occupations or their grandparents' or any other friends or relations. When they are ready, ask them to put their hands up to suggest occupations. Write the occupations on the spare acetate sheet. Try to make the list as long as possible.

There are many different occupations on the list, each one needing different skills. What skills does a lorry driver need? She or he needs to be observant, careful and strong. What skills does a hairdresser need? She or he needs to be very good at using scissors and knowing exactly where to cut hairs. What skills does a doctor need? She or he needs to know about illnesses and how to cure them.

You may wish to focus on some of the other occupations that have been suggested by the children as well.

▦ REFLECTION

You can see that there are many occupations which require many different skills. What skills have you got? Are you good at art, or writing, or number work, or PE, or science? Or are you good at talking to people, or being cheerful and smiling a lot? Everybody is good at something but we are all unique and so we are not all good at the same thing. Everybody is different and everybody is special.

Prayer

Dear God,
Thank you for the skills that we have. Help us to find out what we are good at and help us to use our skills.

Amen

Song

This little light of mine (Alleluya. 14: *A&C Black*)

Andrew Brodie: Assembly Tomorrow KS2 © A&C Black Publishers Ltd. 2008

Occupations

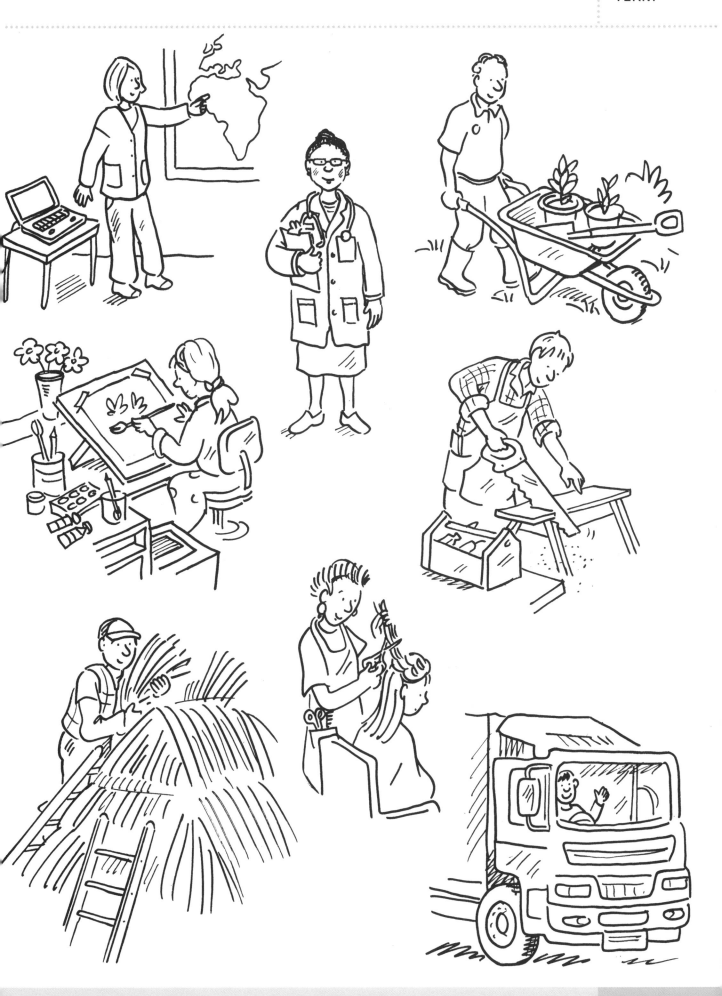

Dog in a manger

 AIM: To remain unselfish and to value other people's needs.

PREPARATION

■ Photocopy 'Dog in a manger 1' and 'Dog in a manger 2' (pages 51 and 52) on to stiff paper or card then cut them out ready to make a simple puppet show.

■ INTRODUCTION

Ask children to indicate by a show of hands whether they know what a manger is. Accept and discuss responses. (Place the silhouette of the manger on the OHP screen.) Explain that we often hear about a manger in the Christmas story. Nowadays it is made of metal and we call it a feeding trough but in years gone by a manger would have been made of wood. This assembly is an Aesop's fable about a dog in a manger.

■ STORY

One day a large dog was looking for a warm, comfortable place to go to sleep. He was a lazy dog and he had had a lazy day. He wandered around the farmyard slowly until he spotted the perfect place where the sun was still shining and, even better, there was a whole pile of comfortable hay to lie on. It was a manger. The dog climbed up into the manger, trampled down the hay, then settled down to sleep. (Put the silhouette of the dog on top of the manger.)

Not long afterwards, a large, hard-working, tired and very hungry ox who had finished his work in the fields, headed for the farmyard. He was looking forward to his evening meal – a great big pile of fresh hay that the farmer would have put in the manger ready for him.

But when he reached the farmyard (put the picture of the ox next to the manger), *he found the large dog lying on his dinner. All the fresh hay was squashed down and didn't look very appetizing but the ox was hungry and started to eat the hay from around the dog.*

The dog woke up and growled loudly. "What are you doing to my bed?" snarled the dog.
"What are you doing to my dinner?" replied the ox.
"Go away," barked the dog. "I was here first. Go away!"
"You are very selfish," said the ox. "You don't want to eat my dinner but you won't let me eat it either."

The ox was frightened of the big angry dog and had no choice but to leave his dinner and to go to bed hungry that night.

■ REFLECTION

What do you think the moral of that story was?

Hopefully someone will suggest that the dog should not have been selfish. They may be able to explain that the dog was depriving the ox of food despite the fact that the food was of no use to him.

Many people are so selfish that they will stop other people from benefiting from something just to be mean to them. Have a quiet think for a minute.

Are you ever selfish? Could you be kinder to other people?

Most of us are a bit selfish sometimes and we must remember to try hard to consider the needs of others.

Prayer

Dear Lord,
Please help us to think of others and not to be selfish. Help us to think of ways in which we can help other people rather than be mean to them.

Amen

Song

It's me, O Lord (Alleluya, 51: *A&C Black*)

 Andrew Brodie: Assembly Tomorrow KS2 © A&C Black Publishers Ltd. 2008

Dog in a manger 1

Dog in a manger 2

Trees

AIM: To encourage pupils to consider the awe and wonder of the natural world and to consider their own lives.

PREPARATION

■ Photocopy the 'Trees' (page 54) on to an acetate sheet to display on the OHP.

INTRODUCTION

Ask the children to identify the main parts of the tree by pointing to the roots, the trunk, the branches and the leaves.

ASSEMBLY

Let's look at the separate parts of the tree. What do the roots do? Why are they there?

Accept responses, ensuring that the children are aware that the roots provide support for the tree and that they gather in water and nutrients from the soil.

We are different from trees because we don't have to stay in one place but we still say that people 'have roots'. So what are our roots?

Accept responses, encouraging ideas such as our homes, our families and our school.

What does the trunk do? Why is it there?

Accept responses, ensuring that the children identify the trunk as the main body of the tree. It gives the tree strength and it carries the water and food up to the branches.

Do we have a trunk? Sometimes our body is called our trunk. Hopefully as we grow up our body gets stronger but we also gain strength in our minds.

What do the branches do? Why are they there?

Accept responses, including the idea that branches hold the leaves and perhaps suggesting that they reach out to the world.

Do we have branches? Perhaps our arms and legs are a bit like branches and they help us to reach out to the world.

What do the leaves do? Why are they there?

Accept responses, ensuring that the children recognize that the leaves gather in the sunlight.

Do we have leaves? No, but perhaps we gather in sunlight and we gather in sights and sounds and we can reach out and touch things.

REFLECTION

Trees are wonderful things. Did you know that we wouldn't be able to breathe without trees? Trees take in carbon dioxide and give out oxygen through their leaves. We can't live without trees because they provide the fresh air for us to breathe.

Prayer

Dear God,
We thank you for the wonderful trees that give us the air to breathe. Help us to to value our roots; help us to grow strong like trees do; help us to reach out to the world, gathering in sights and sounds.

Amen

Song

All things Bright and Beautiful (Come and Praise, 3: *BBC*)

Trees

Say it with flowers

 AIM: To appreciate how flowers, part of the natural world, can brighten up peoples' lives.

PREPARATION

■ Photocopy 'Say it with flowers' (page 56) on to acetate ready to use on an OHP, or you could use a real bunch of flowers.

INTRODUCTION

Introduce the assembly by using the script below or something similar.

Last week a friend of mine ordered a new car from a local garage. When he collected it there was, to his surprise, a large bouquet of flowers on the back parcel shelf. It turned out that this was a present from the garage to say thank you to my friend for buying the car. This made me begin to think about why we buy flowers. The garage had bought them as a thank you gift but people buy flowers for lots of different reasons.

ASSEMBLY

Display 'Say it with flowers' on the OHP and ask the pupils if they can recognize any of the flowers in the picture. Ask the pupils where they have seen flowers for sale and accept all appropriate answers e.g. supermarkets, florists, market stalls, petrol stations, etc.

Now ask why people choose to buy flowers. Again, accept all appropriate responses. In one school answers included: 'at weddings, for brides and bridesmaids to carry'; 'at funerals and in cemeteries'; 'as gifts for birthdays or anniversaries'; 'when people go to visit others'; 'as gifts for patients in hospital to cheer them up'; 'for presentation to actors at the end of a first night of a play'; 'for medal winners at the Olympics' and, of course, 'for themselves to brighten up the homes and to enjoy the fragrance'.

Discuss with pupils which flowers are their personal favourites and why. Ask them to consider how a gift of flowers might make the recipient feel. Answers will include such things as 'flowers make people feel happier', 'flowers make people feel cared about'.

If you have a bunch of real flowers with you encourage them to look at the flowers again and point out to them that each and every flower is unique. No two flowers are identical and this is part of the miracle of God's creation.

REFLECTION

The many types of flower that grow help us to appreciate the natural world. Flowers can cheer us up when we feel low, they can bring the scent of the garden into the home and they seem to bring thoughts and feelings of the outdoors to the inside. They remind us of the miracle of God's creation.

Prayer

Dear Lord,
Thank you Lord for the many beautiful flowers that grow in the world and that we are able to enjoy in our homes. The sight and scents of these flowers brighten our homes and our lives. Flowers remind us of God's wonderful world and his love for us all.

Amen

♪
Song

The flowers that grow in the garden (Someone's Singing Lord, 53: *A&C Black*)
or
English Country Garden (Harlequin, 22: *A&C Black*)

Say it with flowers

Homes

AIM: To understand the importance of having a home that provides shelter and security and the plight of those with no homes.

PREPARATION

■ Photocopy 'Homes' (page 58) ready to present on an OHP.

■ If possible find out a little about any homeless shelters/soup runs, etc. in your local area and any statistics regarding homelessness.

■ Read through the assembly carefully to ensure that you are able to reflect any sensitive issues that may apply in your school situation.

INTRODUCTION

Ask pupils some questions about their homes e.g.

What do you like best about your home? Have you ever moved house and if so how did this make you feel? How do you keep your home warm in the winter?

Accept all answers and focus on feelings of safety, comfort and security that pupils may have in their homes.

ASSEMBLY

Explain that there are many people in this country as well as abroad who have no homes. Every town is likely to have a few people with nowhere to sleep at night. (Show 'Homes' on the OHP.)

Ask if there is anything about the picture that they are surprised to see. This should open up the discussion to the idea that homelessness can happen to anyone – young or old and male or female.

If time allows, ask pupils why they think some people don't have a home to live in. Accept all reasonable answers. Answers could include: some people have left their homes because they have had such unhappiness there, some people have been told that they are no longer welcome in their homes, some people have come from other countries without having a place to live. The pupils may suggest reasons to be homeless in other countries such as war, flood and famine.

Briefly explain that there are charities and organisations that provide emergency shelter for people and charities that take hot food out to the homeless at nights. For example, in this country: Shelter, Oxfam, Salvation Army, Crisis at Christmas and local hostels provide temporary accommodation for the homeless. Other charities around the world include Oxfam, the Red Cross, the Red Crescent and Unicef.

REFLECTION

Those of us with secure happy homes to live in with people who love us are very fortunate. Many people have, for many reasons, nowhere to live. Think quietly for a moment about how you would keep warm, clean and well fed if you had no home to return to each day. Imagine how you and your family would cope if a disaster occurred and resulted in you suddenly having no home.

Prayer

Dear Lord,
We thank you Lord for our homes and families. We thank you too for the people who give their time freely to help those with no homes. We pray for the safety and well being of those who have had difficulties that have led to their being homeless and ask you to help them to find their way to happier lives.

Amen

♪
Song

We're Going Home (Someone's Singing Lord, 59: *A&C Black*)
or
Magic Penny (Alleluya, 10: *A&C Black*)

Homes

Andrew Brodie: Assembly Tomorrow KS2 © A&C Black Publishers Ltd. 2008

A problem shared is a problem halved

 AIM: To help pupils understand the importance of sharing worries.

PREPARATION

- Photocopy 'A problem shared is a problem halved' (page 60) ready to present on the OHP.
- Have markers ready to label the packages on the picture.
- You may also like to gather together some awkward cardboard boxes to demonstrate how difficult they are to carry around.

INTRODUCTION

Tell pupils that everyone has problems from time to time in their lives. Sometimes worries can be small ones that are very easy to sort out. Give examples such as forgetting their packed lunch or their money for a school dinner. Ask pupils how the examples that you have given could be easily rectified.

ASSEMBLY

Ask pupils what sort of problems people might have that would not be easy to resolve. Make it clear that they can suggest problems that both adults and children might have.

Accept all contributions before asking pupils if they can describe what worry feels like. Accept their offers, then show pupils the OHP picture. You could add labels to the parcels to clarify some of the worries. Explain that having problems could be likened to carrying around parcels – the bigger the worry the heavier the parcel. You could invite a pupil to come to the front of the hall and to carry some or all of the cardboard boxes (obviously you will need to check that there is no chance of an injury were any of the boxes to be dropped).

When the child demonstrates how difficult it is to carry all the boxes, ask another child to help carry the load. Next ask pupils how worries can be lessened. Hopefully someone will suggest that talking about a problem can help to deal with it. Ask pupils who, or what, they might share their problems with. Accept all answers including pets and cuddly toys. Point out that sharing the load of boxes made them easier to deal with and, in the same way, sharing problems can make them easier to deal with.

Ask what might prevent them from mentioning their worries to other people. Here the subject of trust will come up. Encourage pupils to think about sharing worries with someone they trust.

REFLECTION

To get the most out of life we need to try to deal with our problems and worries as they occur. To do this we should not be afraid of sharing our worries with people we trust. It is important that we learn to be 'a trusted friend' so that others can share their worries with us without fear of being laughed at. If appropriate you may also decide to mention that there are two large national charities that listen to problems. The ones most pupils will be aware of are 'ChildLine' and the 'Samaritans'.

Prayer

Dear Lord,
Help us to learn to deal with the problems we encounter in life. Help us to understand that everyone has worries during their life and that often sharing the worries we have will help us to be happier. Make us good friends to others, help us to be good listeners when those around us need us to be able to listen to their worries or fears. Please help us always to find someone to share our worries with so that they can help us to deal with the problems that are worrying us.

Amen

Song

When I needed a neighbour (Someone's Singing Lord, 35: *A&C Black*)
or
The Journey of Life (Someone's Singing Lord, 28: *A&C Black*)

A problem shared is a problem halved

The bike accident

AIM: To value the emergency services.

PREPARATION
- Photocopy the 'A bike accident' silhouettes (page 62) on to stiff paper or card and cut them out ready to make a simple puppet show on the OHP.

INTRODUCTION

Today's story is about a boy called Tom who loved playing on his bike. Something happened to him a couple of weeks ago. One minute he was having a good time on his bike, next minute everything changed…

STORY

Tom was out with his friends. They were having a great time, having races on their bikes. They had found a sensible and safe place to ride – a special course of cycle tracks where you could ride up small hills then ride down them again.

Tom was riding really fast and was winning the race, but suddenly his front wheel hit a stone. The wheel twisted round and Tom found himself flying off. He landed with a big bump and his helmet bashed on the ground. For a minute, Tom lost consciousness – he was knocked out. He came round, hearing the voices of his friends:

"Tom, wake up, Tom!"

"Do you think he's all right?"

"Have you got your mobile?"

"I'm going to call 999."

Tom drifted off again and the next thing he knew he was being lifted on to a stretcher by two medics.

"You'll be all right now, son," said a friendly police officer.

Tom was rushed to hospital in the ambulance. When he got there, he was seen by a nurse and a doctor who asked him lots of questions. They decided that he needed to have a head scan to make sure that it wasn't injured inside so he went off with another nurse to the radiography department. He was soon checked out by the radiographer who found that his head was just a bit bruised and said what a good job it was that Tom had been wearing his cycle helmet.

When he got home, his mum showed him his cycle helmet – it had a big dent in it. "Your head could have been like that," she said and she gave him a big hug.

REFLECTION

Now I'm going to read the story again but this time I've got a job for everybody. I would like you to count how many people helped Tom.

Read through the story again, ensuring that everyone who helped is noticed.

Prayer

Dear God,
Thank you for all the people who are there to help us when we are in trouble: our friends, the police, medics, nurses, doctors, radiographers and our own family. Encourage us to value and appreciate all who help and please let us help others when they need us.

Amen

Song

Father I thank you (Everyone's Singing Lord. 4: *A&C Black*)

The bike accident

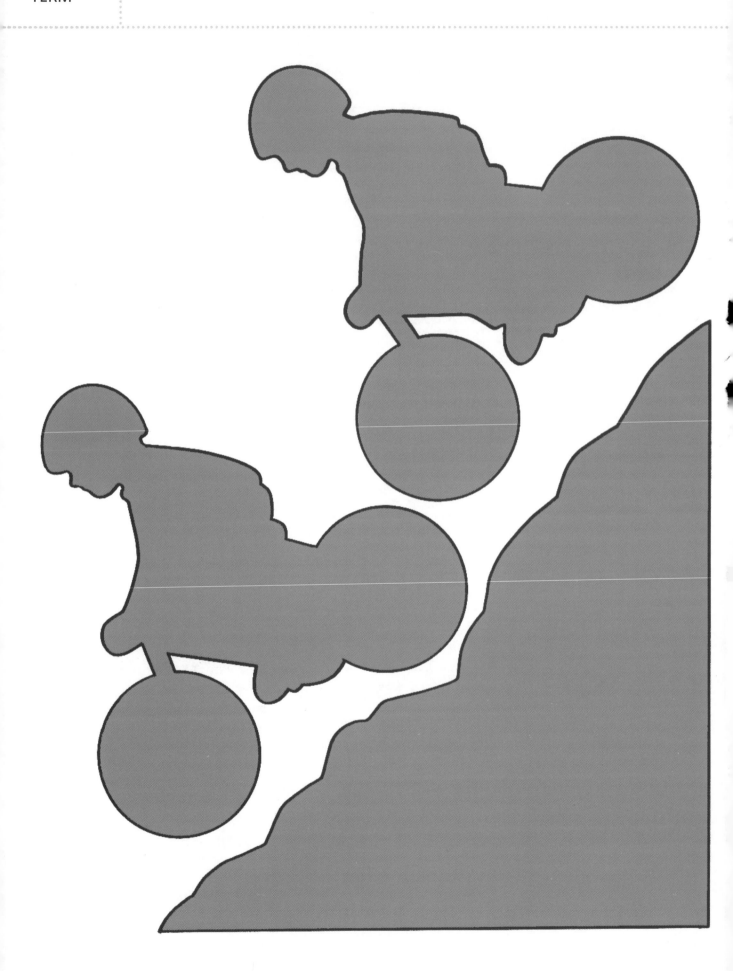

Holidays

➤ **AIM: For pupils to think about all the new and positive experiences that holiday time can bring.**

PREPARATION
■ Photocopy 'Holidays' (page 64) ready for presentation on the OHP.
■ Have a marker pen ready for putting the title on the picture.

■ **INTRODUCTION**

Begin by showing the 'Holidays' picture and asking pupils to suggest a one-word title for the picture. Explain that there is a particular word that you have in mind. When the word 'holidays' has been suggested, write it into the title space and tell pupils that this is what today's assembly will be about.

■ **ASSEMBLY**

First ask pupils what clues helped them to work out that the picture was about holidays. Next ask them what other items they would add to the picture if there was more space. Use their responses, which may be many and varied, to discuss the different types of holiday. This will vary considerably according to the school situation and could be anything from visiting relatives for a day or two to jetting around the world.

Explain to pupils that the word holiday comes from 'holy day' when the only time most people had time off work was for religious celebrations such as saints' days. Tell them that it has only been in recent history that people have enjoyed weekends and holiday breaks. Make sure pupils understand that whilst, for some people, holidays can mean jetting off to other countries, they can also mean enjoying the times when there's no school. This might include days out or being at home with free time to use in whatever way they choose.

As a classroom extension to this activity, the children could draw their own picture clues to represent holidays. Refer back to the initial 'Holidays' picture to ensure that the children do not just produce one picture, but a variety of images which they feel cover a range of holiday experiences.

■ **REFLECTION**

When our school closes for the summer holidays each of us will spend the holiday in different ways. Each day you may have the opportunity to try or learn something new so it is important to make the most of each day. Whilst we all like doing the things that we enjoy most, it is also important to consider the people in our families and friendship groups. We must try to help our friends and family enjoy their holidays too. For example, we could help Mum with some of her jobs or play with a friend who might be lonely.

Prayer

Dear Lord,
We thank you for the holidays we are soon to enjoy: for the new places we might go, the new people we might meet and all the new experiences we will have. Help us to make the most of all these things and to help those around us to enjoy their holidays too.

Amen

Song   The Lord's Day (Alleluya, 4: *A&C Black*)